Deep Prayer

Life Defined by Prayer

Sr Mary David Totah, OSB

*All booklets are published thanks to the
generous support of the members of the
Catholic Truth Society*

CATHOLIC TRUTH SOCIETY
PUBLISHERS TO THE HOLY SEE

Contents

The Nature of Prayer

There is a story of a Frenchman who was very good at escaping from prisoner of war camps. When asked how he did it, he said, "when one is escaping there must always be two." The same thing can be said of prayer; when one is praying there must always be two. Prayer can seem one-sided, but it never is. It's about maintaining a relationship with God; it can almost be called spousal. Here it is not a question of drawing God to us, since God is closer to us than we are to ourselves. Its purpose is to bring us closer to Him. "If we were on a ship, and to rescue us, ropes attached to a rock were thrown to us, obviously we would not draw the rock nearer to ourselves, but we would pull ourselves and our ship nearer to the rock. And that is why in prayer we need to begin not by drawing to ourselves that Power that is everywhere and nowhere, but by putting ourselves into his hands and uniting ourselves to him" (Dionysius the Areopagite, c. 500, Divine Names, III). Prayer is the journey to the kingdom: the arrival is union with God.

This understanding of prayer can help us to grasp its real content and meaning, and awaken us to its larger context. There is always a danger of bringing down prayer too much to the level of everyday life, to think of it only a kind of mental refreshment, a mental hygiene, a source of personal enrichment. Prayer is of course a part of life; but the contemporary stress on quiet time and breathing techniques which can be a help can also deflect us from the true dimensions of prayer. We might be led into thinking only in terms of personal development, but the real question must always be: how far does my prayer open my mind and heart to God.

Here is it is important to be aware of what we believe as Christians, the greater context of our prayer. The Catechism opens with a great affirmation that man is a religious being; he belongs to another order, another dimension. We have here no abiding city, and even in the most insignificant moments of our life we belong to another world. What we feel, hear, see, touch is not all there is. Prayer is born of the conviction that the world we live in is not two-dimensional; it is born of the conviction that we are surrounded by an invisible world, that God is our supreme reality and deepest truth. There is something of eternity in us; we have a capacity or God. We have a capacity to know God and receive his revelation, because we are made in the image of God, and because God has revealed himself to us.

This brings us to a second point. God has come to us, spoken to us in human terms in the human nature of Christ. Von Balthasar has said: "Religion is the world in its journey towards God. Christianity is God journeying towards the world." Christianity is a religion of revelation; it proclaims that God's love is always drawing near to man. Christian prayer, steeped in *Lectio divina* and liturgy, marked by a profoundly Scriptural character, is carried out in an aura of revelation. Salvation history is the context of the Christian's daily life.

This transforms everything: the practical problem of our response to life, our relationship with God, our notion of prayer. Prayer is no longer a feeble attempt on our part to speak to the Creator. In the Incarnation the Creator has spoken to us and given us a guide in our efforts to respond. We pray as those who have been found by God. Prayer has been transformed by Christ from a desperate cry in the night to a *response*, springing from deep within, a response that is love, a response that is free to speak to the Father as the heart prompts us. Indeed compared with other developed religions, the prayer of petition would seem to be uniquely Christian. We see this in our Lord himself, always turning towards the Father in childlike receptivity for his will and his gifts.

That is why the most important thing is that we give time to prayer. Here it is not a question of finding time but of *offering* time. Nothing is more precious than our time. Prayer is a way of spending time specifically set apart for God, an offering of a space in your day that you make to the Father. It is time given, burnt, offered as a holocaust, a time when self and problems are deliberately forgotten so that you may be open, available to God. This in itself is an act of faith, of love, an act of will and conviction, the holocaust of ourselves. "Prayer is keeping company with God" (Cyril of Alexandria).

Prayer is by nature a dialogue between man and God. It unites the soul with its Creator and reconciles the two. Its effect is to hold the world together.

(St John Climacus)

The only way to pray is to pray; and the way to pray well is to pray much. If one has no time for this, then one must at least pray regularly. But the less one prays, the worse it goes.

(Dom John Chapman)

A Life Characterized by Prayer

Prayer should be seen as a dimension of a whole life lived perseveringly for God. What matters is not so much constantly increasing the amount of prayer but that we incorporate the practice of prayer in the rhythm of our daily living. This booklet will help to show how this may be done.

Often we think that to pray means to say prayers. But in reality, prayer is not so much an activity as a state. To be in a state of continual prayer, it is not necessary to recite an unending series of prayers, for there is such a thing as implicit continual prayer. Certainly the repetition of a short formula (more about which later) is an excellent way of seeking to attain this implicit state. But there may come a point when the state of prayer continues even though the repetition does not; when the formula, instead of being something we have continually to say, somehow passes into the very fibre of our being, so that even when it is not said it is still always there. In this sense there are people who pray even when they sleep; for they pray, not primarily by virtue of anything they say or think, but rather by virtue of what they are. St Basil the Great makes this point in his homily on the martyr Julitta:

"We should not express our prayer merely in syllables, but the power of prayer should be expressed in the moral attitude of our soul and in the virtuous actions that extend through out our life ... This is how you pray continually -not by offering prayer in words, but in joining yourself to God through you whole way of life, so that your life becomes one continuous and uninterrupted prayer."

Do not reduce your prayer to words; make the totality of your life a prayer to God" (Isaac the Syrian)

This state of prayer is not so much the culmination of a lifetime of saying prayers or giving oneself to the practice of meditation; it is rather the natural outcome of a whole way of life dedicated to openness to grace, to faith in the divine presence and the working of providence in our lives. A particular state of prayer is not sought directly; the Christian seeks God not experiences. It springs readily and unself-consciously to one who does his best to respond to the call of grace in every circumstance, and to put into practice the Gospel in concrete behaviour. It is the result of the commitment to persevere in the attempt irrespective of where such commitment leads. What counts in life and in prayer is the our voluntary gift of ourselves in the love of Christ, not the enjoyment of spiritual gifts.[1] The Christian seeks God not experiences; he lives in the luminous twilight of faith.

The key to prayer, then, is the quality of daily life. Prayer is a dimension of one's whole life, realised differently in different occupations. Prayer should not be an activity existing in competition with other activities; growth in prayer is not necessarily facilitated by the withdrawal from other activities. Every action can be directed towards God. To pray well we need a lifestyle that not only allocates time for prayer but also knows how to use other times wisely. The question is not whether to pray, but how to make best use of the opportunities provided. Of course there will be moments when prayer seems less diffuse and more concentrated, but that is a question of difference of degree rather than of two distinct activities.

Prayer is not just part of a Christian's life; it is the structure of his life, and after a lifetime, it becomes the very structure of his being. Prayer is not just an activity added to other activities; it is the condition of his being out of which all his actions spring.

---

[1] "Modern man seeks mainly for 'experience'-putting himself at the centre of things, he wishes to make them subservient to this aim; too often even God becomes the source from which the highest experience flows, instead of being Him Whom we adore , worship, and are prepared to serve whatever the cost to us. Such an attitude was unknown in the desert ... [which was rather} an endeavour to respond to love for love. And this response is the ascetic endeavour ..." (Metropolitan Anthony Bloom, Foreword to *Sayings of the Desert Fathers*, ed Benedicta Ward).

Prayer must penetrate and enliven every department of life, including that which is most temporal and transient. Prayer does not despise even the seemingly lowliest aspects of man's temporal existence. It gives them all a divine orientation.

(Thomas Merton)

If prayer is bound up with our life then it follows that our prayer will be a reflection of our daily living. What we experience in prayer can never be at odds with objective norms: in other words if our prayer is leading us to live a life of greater love and self-forgetfulness, then it comes from God. If it leads to laxity, arrogance, excesses, lack of prudence, then these feelings do not come from God. It is for this reason John Cassian (c 360-430) says that if you find prayer unsatisfactory, then maybe you should look at your life: "For whatever the soul was thinking about before the time of prayer inevitably occurs to us when we pray as a result of the operation of the memory. Hence we must prepare ourselves before the time of prayer to be the prayerful persons we wish to be. For the mind in prayer is shaped by the state that it was previously in, and when we sink into prayer, the image of the same deeds, words, and thoughts plays itself out before our eyes" (Conferences 9:3). Cassian is advocating a life lived in progressive mindfulness of God, in which pursuits foreign to one's goal are gradually eliminated. In this way the heart becomes more pure and single.

Most of our conflicts and difficulties in prayer come from trying to deal with the spiritual and practical aspects of our life separately, instead of seeing them as parts of one whole. If our practical life is centred on our own interests, cluttered up by possessions, distracted by ambitions, passions, desires and worries, beset by a sense of our own rights and importance or anxieties about the future or longings for our own success, we cannot expect our prayer life to be any different. That is why the ancient teaching on prayer lay such great stress on interior combat, freeing the soul and purifying the heart, and spiritual renunciation and discipline, to fight resolutely against deeply rooted habits and inclinations that are the result of sin, both original and personal.

Linking prayer and life can be a source of hope. First, because if the quality of our prayer is determined by the way we live, this means that striving to live a more evangelical life we are moving towards an ever more profound experience of God. Prayer is a union of wills, to be "oned" with God (Julian of Norwich). And this is accomplished through our habitual and heartfelt assent to the manifestations of God's will in our nature, our personal history, the duties of our life, and the many

11

areas of challenge by which we are invited to move towards greater love. This is how our wills become aligned to God's, step by step; in touch with God, or rather touched at every moment by God. In his book *On the Love of God*, St. Bernard shows that a total experience of God (ecstasy) involving a total transcendence of self begins at a very mundane level; not a matter of some esoteric learning or practising some special asceticism. It is learning to live in self-forgetfulness, going beyond oneself in compassion and self-giving.

This connection between prayer and life also means that prayer is going to share something of the vicissitudes of life itself. This changeable character of life is something that continues throughout life and is bound to affect our prayer. As John Cassian noted, "It is absolutely certain that no one's prayers can be uniform. For a person prays one way when he is happy and another way when he is burdened by a weight of sadness or despair; one way when he is enjoying spiritual successes and another way when he is oppressed by numerous attacks; one way when he is begging pardon for sins and another way when his is asking for grace or some virtue ... ." (Conf. 9:8.) In Conference 10:10 Cassian describes how prayer can ring a wide range of changes, can possess a wide variety of qualities, even though the same prayer is used. It is logical, however, that our choice of prayer form will also be subject to variation, according to the seasons of our lives and fluctuations of recent circumstances and experiences. All kinds of feelings -anger, distraction, sadness- flood in to make our attempts at prayer difficult. This is natural, we must anticipate that this may happen, and so come to prayer with the idea that a struggle or resistance may be necessary. I will be talking about some of the trials we find in prayer and some strategies later.

The point here is that like our Christian life, Christian prayer is going to involve participating in the paschal mystery of Christ. We have to accept death sometimes in order to rise to newness of life. Trying to avoid such death is likely to lead to prayerlessness: just as in life, such avoidance leads to escapism, a lack of depth or commitment. "The less one prays the worse it goes" (Dom John Chapman). Like Christian life, prayer needs the dimension of faith, the conviction that God is acting in and through all the circumstances of our life. In commenting on the Lord's prayer, Cassian says that our ability to pray is connected with our acceptance of God's providence in our regard: "No one will really be able to say this [Thy will be done on earth as it is in heaven] but him who believes that God regulates all things that are seen, whether fortunate or unfortunate, for the sake of our well-being, and that he is more provident and careful with regard to the salvation and interests of those who are his own than we are for ourselves" (Conference 9:20). Do we believe God acts in the events in our life? To the extent that we do not, negative things will play havoc with our emotional life, and generate anger, sadness, or accidie[2] -the great obstacles to prayer according to Cassian. If on the other hand we have faith in God's working through the daily events, we will be better able to let go, more drawn to greater self-forgetfulness, acts of forgiveness, service. Our prayer in turn will remain fresh, and our life will become more supple, causing prayer to flow more freely, not only at regular slots but unexpectedly as well. Again we find the continuity between prayer and life: what happens outside prayer, noted the ancient monks, is going to determine the quality of our prayer. That's why they give no detailed guidance about techniques. There's nothing abstract about all this; far from being an exercise in greater abstraction, prayer becomes a matter of growing closer to the person of Christ. Very little fuss or fanfare: just continuing fidelity to theological virtues, good living,

---

[2] Accidie is despondency, listlessness, a distaste for life for no specific reason; it can manifest itself as a refusal to take seriously the challenge of the moment, an attitude of habitually tending towards the easier and less demanding option, minimising obligations.

patience, humility, learning to live in the context of God's love and providence. Ordinary, yet demanding, close to the Gospel.

If we wish our prayers to penetrate not only the heavens but what is even above the heavens, we should make an effort to draw our mind, purged of every earthly vice and cleansed of all the dregs of the passions, back to its natural lightness, so that thus its prayer might ascend to God, unburdened by the weight of any vice.

(John Cassian)

An Environment for Prayer: the Bible and the Liturgy

Lectio Divina

Those who want to give themselves more fully to prayer are often most interested in practicalities. How do I do it? How do I pray or mediate or reach contemplation? The foundation, the first phase, of all the activity of prayer was for the ancients *Lectio Divina*, or sacred reading. This consisted in a special way of reading (*Lectio*). It is called *Divina* because its object was sacred Scripture. But for the Catholic Church Scripture is never separated from interpretation given to it by tradition. So *Lectio* embraces not only the Bible but also commentaries written on it by the Fathers of the Church. This is the *content* of *Lectio*. But *Lectio* also denotes above all a *method* of reading, a slow, contemplative reading which allows the word of God to become a means of union with God. Such holy reading was both a preparation for prayer and prayer itself.

Lectio prepares or provokes a personal contact with the Lord. At a given moment, we close the book and our eyes, and open our soul to God in intimate dialogue: a dialogue that can consist of silence or only a few words. It is a dialogue consisting in uniting ourselves to God through the words we have read, tasted, savoured, loved. In this way, reading and prayer are but two stages of one and the one process: "we speak to Him when we pray; He speaks to us when we read", as St Jerome and others loved to say. Note the two movements here: to converse, it is necessary to listen, then speak. *Lectio* than becomes the subject matter of prayer. The soul speaks to the Bridegroom by borrowing the same words of Scripture she's been reading. *Lectio* is no dry exercise; there is a real concern to hear Christ, to make him present by means of the biblical texts.

Monastic tradition distinguished four stages in the practice of *Lectio*: reading, meditation, prayer, contemplation.

(a) *Lectio*, the reading properly speaking, the attentive reading of the text, a way of reading the text for itself and not by relying on a commentary.

(b) *Meditatio* (pondering). For Biblical, as for patristic and medieval ages, *meditatio* was a murmuring, a recitation, saying the text aloud, so that it could be kept and savoured. Keeping a text in the heart serves as a reminder of God's intervention and presence in our life. Texts of Scripture carried around in the memory allow God's word to speak to each situation as it occurs. The recitation of Scripture is a powerful way of restoring focus, unity of mind and heart. As William of St Thierry wrote:

"Some part of your daily reading should each day be stored in the stomach (i.e. memory) and be allowed to be digested. At times it should be brought up again for frequent rumination. You should select something that is in keeping with your calling and in line with your personal orientation, something that will seize hold of your mind and not allow it to think over alien matters." (Golden Ep. 31:120)

This is the stage for reading out loud, writing bits out, learning bits off by heart and reciting them at various moments later in the day.[3] The ancients appreciated far more than we do the role that memory can play in prayer. It was expected that every well-equipped Christian would carry about with him a stock of favourite scriptural texts from which he could select

---

[3] What is interesting here is that according to tradition there can be no meditation without a previous or simultaneous reading. Just as there is no liturgy without Scripture so there is no meditation without Scripture.

food for thought and forms of prayer as the occasion warranted. This act of memorization was not a form of brainwashing, nor was it akin to the disembodied verbal sequences used by some modern cults. What was preserved in the memory was the word of God; it was "treasured up in the heart", after the example of Our Lady; it mediated God's will, and gave them strength.

(c) *Oratio* (prayer). As a response to the reading, the *oratio* can express itself in various ways: as thanksgiving, supplication, contrition, etc. In the reading God has spoken to us; here we speak to Him, respond to the divine word which he has recited. Prayer arises almost effortlessly when the two previous activities have been made. The object of reading is to provoke prayer.

(d) *Contemplatio*. A quiet resting in God, a waiting upon God, a gazing upon God: "I look at Him and He looks at me, and we are happy together" (a peasant to St John Vianney). No one who has ever been in love needs to be reminded that there are moments when words are unnecessary. It is the same in our relationship with God. This stage is to rest in the experience of being in the presence of God.

Elaborating on the verse from the psalm, "Taste and see," Guigo the Carthusian compared *reading* to the act of bringing a morsel of food to the mouth; *meditation* to the process of biting and chewing the morsel; *prayer* is swallowing it, bringing it into the interior of the heart and beginning to savour it; finally in *contemplation* we enjoy the sweetness that delights and refreshes. These four stages describe the process of *Lectio*; but they are not four steps in a recipe that have to be followed each time. They merely describe what happens when the reader contacts the word. The whole process is a method of prayer

Here is the 12th c. English Cistercian St Aelred of Rievaulx's Lectio on the Gospel of Annunciation:

First enter the room of blessed Mary and with her read the books that prophesy the virginal birth and the coming of Christ. Wait there for the arrival of the angel, so that you may see him as he comes in, hear him as he utters his greeting and so, filled with amazement, greet your sweet Lady together with the angel. Cry with a loud voice, 'hail full of grace the Lord is with you, blessed are you among women.' Repeat this several times and consider what this fullness of grace is, in which the whole world shared when the Word was made flesh and dwelt among us, full of grace and truth. Wonder at the Lord who fills heaven and earth being enclosed within the womb of

a maiden, whom the Father sanctified, the Son
made fruitful and the Holy Spirit overshadowed.[4]

There is nothing sentimental in the meditation on this text; rather there is rapture before the mystery, wonder and amazement born of close attention to the Gospel scene; a flexible and spontaneous mingling of vocal and contemplative prayer, of reflection on the mystery of the Incarnation and the action of the Trinity. Note too Aelred's stress on repeating the words.

In this practice, we soon discover that a familiar text can be used to stir up prayer, or help us in difficult times. Letting the Word of God flow in and out of the mind develops in us an aptitude for prayer that leads to a real renewal of our lives. We learn to clarify our situation in the light of God's word, and seek after virtue. Many sins and ambiguities fall away. Continuous exposure to the word of God in *Lectio* can keep us from confusing ultimate values and our own subjective experience; it is a great preparation for the prayers which the Christian seeks to build into his life.

Prayer and Liturgical Life

It is significant that in the Rule of St Benedict intimate prayer follows naturally upon the celebration for the

---

[4] Rule of life for a Recluse (his sister) 29, Cistercian Publications, 1971.

liturgy. Personal prayer for the Christian should be closely linked to Mass and the Liturgy of the Hours, whether in order to prepare for it or to prolong it. Dom Delatte called the liturgy "organised contemplation"; it is the Church's contemplation, the song of Spouse to her Bridegroom as she gazes on him. The Word of God teaches us to tend towards contemplation, to cultivate interior recollection, and to practise loving attention to God. And participation in the Mass, the sacraments and the Liturgy of the Hours is one of the best preparations for union with God by contemplation. One of the signs that Mass or another liturgical service has been well-celebrated is that it gives rise to the desire to pray, to savour the sweetness of what has taken place, to rest without words in the presence of the living God. The goal of prayer is ultimately union with God. In baptism, the sacraments, above all in the Eucharist, God gives us in the Church all the objective conditions we need for union with him, all the means we need for the attainment of that end. The whole of the life of prayer is a deepening and realisation of Eucharistic communion with Christ. On our side, of course, we must produce the necessary subjective conditions, for it is in this co-operation that union is fulfilled.

The liturgy is a great school of Prayer. It is part of this environment of prayer and can provide the structured means by which a prayerful life is supported. We are initiated into prayer by the prayers, psalms, hymns of the Church, the Mass of each day, the great poem of the liturgy which spreads itself out throughout the year. The Liturgy of the Hours has been compared to a drip putting a steady flow of nutrient into a person's system. The story of our journey to the Kingdom is what is bring celebrated every liturgical year from Advent to Pentecost, and it is that story which gives meaning to our time, to the drama of our lives, with its defeats and victories. The different times of the year feel different, have their different melodies, different colours -which can do so much to help us in our own prayer. The liturgy is a great school of prayer for it involves a dedication of the will, the renunciation of other thoughts and expectations; it is a waiting on God which is full of love. The liturgy is part of the proper human response to God's self-revelation, to his entering into a relationship with us.

We find this close relationship between liturgy and contemplation in the life and work of St Gertrude. Dom Guéranger brings out this unity in his introduction to his edition of her Exercises: "This holy daughter of the cloister drank in light and life day by day from the sources of all true contemplation, from the very fountain of living waters which gushes forth from the psalms and the inspired words of the Divine Office. Her every sentence shows how exclusively her soul was nourished with this heavenly food. She so lived in the liturgy that we continually find in her revelations that the Saviour discloses to her the mysteries of heaven, and the Mother of God and the saints hold converse with her on some antiphon, or response or introit, which the Saint is singing with delight, and of which she is striving to feel all the force and sweetness." He also notes the breadth and liberty in this ancient method of prayer.

"For the contemplative liturgical prayer is sometimes the source , sometimes the result of the Lord's visits."

(Dom Guéranger)

The Practice
of Prayer

Continual meditation on the living word of God in the Bible and liturgy inevitably fills the heart and mind with a reservoir of sacred thoughts and images. This kind of meditation is a prayer in its own right. No clear cut boundaries divide reading and meditation from another activity of the spirit, contemplation. Although some books of prayer seek to suggest mental prayer is higher and better than vocal prayer, it is not easy, or desirable, to divide prayer into separate degrees, and all such systematising is relative. Prayer is a living relationship between persons, and personal relationships cannot be neatly classified. The various kinds of prayer we are about to describe are not so much successive as simultaneous. We are to think of the life of prayer, vocal or mental, in terms of deepening levels, interdependent, coexisting with each other. However one might distinguish between reading, prayer, meditation, the liturgy, the one interpenetrates the others so powerfully in actual practice that it is more a matter of varying degrees of intensity of contact with the Word than a matter of four or five distinct realities. For as the ancients understood so well, the Word is present in various ways, in Scripture surely, in Christ fully, in the Church, in the sacraments. Whether chanting the psalms, receiving the Eucharist, doing spiritual reading, praying in the silence of one's heart while working, the Christian is celebrating the mystery of Christ.

Words are important in prayer, even if later they may give way to a more silent prayer. Our Lord gave us the Our Father as a typical prayer (Matthew 6:9-13; Luke 11:2-4). Nor is it artificial or impersonal to use existing forms of prayer to God. It is often assumed that spontaneity is the mark of sincerity. Nevertheless there are times when the expression of our feelings is very carefully phrased, even when addressing someone to whom we are very close: a declaration of affection or a humble apology. And one of the effects of original sin is that our spontaneous reactions are not always in line with what is right and true, or even in line with what, at our deepest level, we really intend. Existing forms of prayer can help shape our spiritual attitudes and feelings. We go to galleries and concerts to learn what real music and real art is, to form our taste, and this is partly why we should not hesitate to use set prayers, to learn which feelings, thoughts, and expressions are used by those in the Church.

Arrow prayers

Abba Macarius was asked, 'How should one pray?'
The old man said, "There is no need at all to make
long discourses; it is enough to stretch out one's
hands and say. "Lord, as you will, and as you know,
have mercy.' And if the conflict grows fiercer say,
"Lord, help!' He knows very well what we need and
he shows us his mercy.

(Sayings of the Desert Fathers)

The desert fathers strove primarily for prayer without
ceasing, sustained by frequent brief prayers, sometimes
condensed into a single formula. The repetition of a
short sentence exemplified Jesus in the Garden whom
we are told repeated the same words over and over
again (*Mt* 26:44). Even the prayer of the Spirit in us is
limited to a single cry: Abba Father. Jesus himself
taught his disciples not to squander a lot of words in
prayer. This simple way of prayer quickly found its way
into the tradition. The Fathers called it "monologia," a
prayer consisting of a few words, or even only of one
word. The desert monk Arsenius liked: "God lead me in
the way of salvation." Apollo's favourite was: "I have
sinned like a man; like God have mercy." Cassian liked
best the verse from the psalm: "God come to my aid,
Lord hasten to help me." John Climacus: "Let your

prayer be simple and without many words. One word was enough to procure forgiveness from the tax-collector and the prodigal son ... A single word saved the good thief. Lengthy prayers build up all sorts of images in the mind and distract it, whereas a single word can bring it to a state of recollection. If you feel that by uttering a word you are inwardly comforted and mollified, stay with that word, for then your angel is praying with you" (Ladder 28). In the Institutes Cassian says, anticipating the ninth and tenth conferences: "The father think it best if prayers are short but offered frequently. They should be frequent so that by praying often we may be able to cleave to God without ceasing. They should be short so that we may avoid the assaults of the devil, who threatens us particularly when we are at prayer" (II, 10). Cassian comes back to this point in Conference IX, 36.

Augustine also refers to this practice in his letter to Proba:

"We are told that in Egypt there are brothers who offer up frequent prayers , but that these are very short, like arrows loosed off in rapid succession, for fear that that vigilant alert attention so necessary for one who prays, should be weakened or blunted if too long an interval is left between them. Thus they show quite clearly that our attention is not to be forced if it cannot be prolonged, while on the other hand it should not be quickly broken off it is capable of being prolonged. So a multiplicity of words should be absent from prayer, but as long as ardent attention remains, let there be frequent supplications ... Praying intensely means repeatedly and fervently stirring the heart, knocking at the door of him to whom we are praying." (Letter 130, 19-20).

In these ways we concentrate and unify our ever-active minds by nourishing it on a spiritual diet at once exceedingly simple and rich. As John Cassian urged, reduce prayer to the poverty of a simple word or phrase.

Lectio is important here, for many brief ejaculatory prayers in the Bible may be used for prayer. The Gospels and the psalms are a goldmine. "Lord Jesus, I believe; help my unbelief; Lord Jesus, that I may see; Lord you know that I love you; Not my will, but yours." The list is endless, and each saying, each word is inexhaustible. The Fathers would say: So long as one of these formulas keeps your heart going, do not drop it, quietly persist until your heart is totally on fire within, the moment God so pleases.

Elsewhere in the Conferences, Abba Isaac comments on the remarkable power available to the monk from ceaselessly reciting this verse from the psalms, "O God make speed to save me, O Lord make haste to help me" (*Ps* 69:2). Although this is only one of many verses a monk might utter during meditation, it is particularly useful for illustrating the power of meditation: "It can be adapted to every condition and can usefully be deployed against every temptation" (Conference 10:10). Abba Isaac goes on to note that the mind, in grasping a single verse of Scripture, will be able to "cast away the wealth and multiplicity of other thoughts, and restore itself to the poverty of a single verse." The recitation of Scripture was held to unify the mind, helping it to overcome dissipation and distraction which leaves it open to various attacks of the demons.

This practice of short, ejaculatory prayers helps us, then, to combat hurtful or simply irrelevant thoughts; and on the positive side, these prayers are at the service of a perpetual remembrance of God. "Pray always" (*Lk* 18:11), "in all seasons" (*Eph* 6:18), "without ceasing" (1 *Thess* 5:17); these recommendations are embedded in Scripture and are to be taken seriously. It is physically and psychologically impossible to engage in specific acts of prayer without interruption; but through these short prayers we strive for an approximate state, a disposition of heart which can in a real way be called prayer; the perpetual remembrance of God, a habit of heart, the expression of a love that always tends toward the thought of the beloved even when it must attend to something else.

These short formulas enable us to bridge the gap between more explicit times of prayer -whether at church services or alone in our room- and going about our business during the day: "It is possible to offer fervent prayer even while walking in public ... or seated in you shop, while buying or selling, even while cooking" (St John Chrysostom). As St Teresa of Avila said "the Lord walks among the pots and pans ... The true lover everywhere loves his beloved and continually remembers him. It would be a bad business if we were able to practise prayer only when alone in corners." These short prayers, help us to stand in the presence of God wherever we are. So we become like Br Lawrence of the Resurrection (1611-1691) who "was more united with God during his ordinary activities than in religious exercises." It is a great delusion," he remarked, "to imagine that prayer-time should be different from any other, for we are equally bound to be united to God by work at work-time as by prayer at prayer-time."

The shorter the word the better, being more like the working of the Spirit. A word like 'God' or 'Love'. Choose which you like, so long as it is of one syllable.

And fix this word fast to your heart, so that it is always there, come what may. It will be your shield and spear in peace and war alike.

(The Cloud of Unknowing)

The Jesus Prayer

At the beginning of the 5th century a privileged place began to be given to the invocation of the name of Jesus, "Lord Jesus Christ, Son of God, have mercy on me." The verbal formula may be shortened: we can say "Lord Jesus Christ have mercy on me," "Lord Jesus," or sometimes, less commonly, the name of Jesus alone. It is the short prayer most favoured among Eastern Christians, though it was not unknown in the West. "The manifold repetition of the name," wrote St Aelred to his sister in the 12th century, "pierces our heart from within." As the Russian Pilgrim affirms, the Jesus Prayer "holds in itself the whole Gospel truth"; it is "a summary of the Gospels." In one brief sentence, it embodies the two great mysteries of the Christian faith, the Incarnation and the Trinity. It speaks of the two natures of Christ as God and man, for he is invoked first by the human name Jesus, which his mother Mary gave him at birth, and then by his eternal Godhead, for he is also called Lord and Son of God. The prayer also implies the Trinity. While addressing the Son, it also points to the Father and can only be said in the Holy Spirit, for "no one can say Lord Jesus except in the holy Spirit" (1 *Cor* 12:3).

Devotionally too, the Jesus prayer embraces the two key moments that should characterise all Christian prayer -the moment of adoration, of looking to God's glory and reaching out to him in love; and the moment of repentance, the consciousness of unworthiness and sin. In the first half of the prayer we rise up to God: "Lord Jesus Christ, Son of God." In the second half we return to ourselves in compunction: "Have mercy on me a sinner." "Mercy" bridges the gulf between God and fallen man.

The Jesus Prayer is considered a particularly effective invocation because of the intrinsic power and virtue of the divine Name. In the Bible to invoke a person's name is to make that person present. How much more is this true of the divine Name. God's name is essentially linked with his person. For the believing Christian today, as in apostolic times, the Name of Jesus is power. Again, like other short prayers drawn from the Bible or liturgy, the Jesus prayer is not hypnotic incantation or a magic talisman; we are to invoke the Name with recollection and reverence, mindful of who it is we are addressing.

When we have blocked all the outlets of the mind by means of the remembrance of God, then it requires of us at all costs some task which will satisfy its need for activity. Let us give it then as its sole activity the prayer, "Lord Jesus. ..."

(Diadochus of Photike, 5th c.)

Through the remembrance of Jesus, gather together your scattered mind.

(Philotheos of Sinai, 9th-10th c.)

The Name of the Son of God is great and boundless, and upholds the entire universe.

(The Shepherd of Hermas)

The Rosary

The rosary might be called "the Mary prayer", a form of praying that leads us into the contemplation of the mystery of salvation in which Mary is intimately united with he work of her Son. Pope John Paul II in his Apostolic Letter *Rosarium Virginis Mariae* explicitly connects the rosary to the tradition we have been tracing: "The rosary belongs among the finest and most praiseworthy traditions of Christian contemplation. Developed in the West, it is a typically meditative prayer, corresponding in some way to the 'prayer of the heart' or 'Jesus prayer' which took root in the soil of the Christian East." And like the Jesus Prayer, it is a compendium of the Gospel. Contemplating Christ through Mary in the rosary is above all a "remembering." In early patristic centuries, contemplation was thought of as remembering

34

God in his creative and redemptive activity. For Scripture and the early Fathers, such remembering already includes an element of personal engagement. "I ponder all your works," says the psalmist (*Ps* 118) "Think on these things," St Paul advises the Philippians, and in St. Luke's Gospel, the mother of Christ herself "kept all these things and pondered them in her heart." And this remembering is a form of making present: "These events not only belong to 'yesterday'; *they are also part of the today of salvation*... to 'remember' them in a spirit of faith and love is to be open to the grace which Christ won for us by the mysteries of his life, death and resurrection" (Pope John Paul II).

Each decade of the rosary opens with the Our Father. In the Our Father we ask for the fundamental object of all Christian prayer, the Kingdom; in the rosary we contemplate the mysteries in which the Kingdom is shown forth to us. The Angelic salutation, the first part of the Hail Mary, proclaims how the Kingdom became interior in the one who was full of grace. The second part of the prayer speaks of the way Mary's interior appropriation of the Kingdom is to be transferred to ourselves. "Holy Mary, Mother of God, pray for us ..." We are invited to have Christ and his mysteries not just before our eyes but in our hearts as we open ourselves to the plan of God for us, a plan which shall have its fulfilment "at the hour of our death."

The Our Father

Jesus Christ left us only one prayer, which is therefore usually called the Lord's prayer. When the disciples implored him, "teach us to pray (*Lk* 11:1) , he gave them this prayer in reply. In it a complete description of what Christian prayer should be: its character and object; its balance, quality and tone. In the seven clauses of the Lord's prayer we have seven lessons in prayer, seven fundamental moments in a single act of communion between ourselves and the Father.

> *Run through all the words of the holy prayers in Scripture, and I do not think that you will find anything in them that is not contained and included in the Lord's Prayer.*
>
> (St Augustine, Epistle 130; cited in CCC 2762)

Our Father who art in heaven: The first thing Christ teaches us as a priceless gift and consolation is the possibility of calling God Father. This first invocation establishes our place before God, not merely as his creatures but as his children. We are sons and daughters of the Eternal Father, inheritors of heaven; we have in us a spark of divine life. As the Catechism reminds us, heaven is not so much a place as a way of being, God's presence in the hearts of the just (cf. CCC

2794-2796). "Heaven is God and God is in my soul," said Elizabeth of the Trinity. This opening petition is the foundation of the prayer, making all the other petitions possible.

Hallowed be thy name: This is the cry of selfless adoration; of someone who recognises the primacy of God. Indeed the very reason for the Church's existence is the more perfect hallowing of God's name. In the first petition we express our childlike and loving relation to God; in this second, our unlimited awe before his mystery, a mystery that grows deeper the nearer we approach. Our prayer must always bring with it a certain sense of how much remains unseen. The sanctification of God's name in the world depends inseparably on our prayer and our life. May everything in the world, beginning with my own life, my words and deeds, my contacts and relationships, my struggles and temptations, thoughts and desires be shaped by this loving reverence. There can be no limit to this consecration of life, putting the Holy first. This petition reminds us that our life and work are meaningful only insofar as they glorify God, and the rest of the prayer unfolds the different ways in which this adoring response can be made more complete.

Thy Kingdom come: In the New Testament, this word can be translated as kingship or kingdom or reign. After acknowledging the priority of holiness, we now pray that God's purposes, great or small, may be realised in us; it is a renunciation of our own natural sovereignty and a total acceptance of his rule of love in our lives. This will mean enduring, even welcoming, God's transforming power in our lives; and more actively, a self-offering for the purposes of the Kingdom, eager and active service involving the use of created things- money, time, position, dedicating our powers to bring about the reign of God in individual hearts. Our praying life must lead to an active and self-sacrificing co-operation with God.

Thy will be done on earth as it is in heaven: With this prayer, we are brought to a more complete self-opening to God; our will is given to us that it may be united in love to Him from whom it came. And this is something to be realised in the homely experiences and humble duties of daily life. We ask here for the grace of abandonment to the mysterious divine purposes, recognising and welcoming his action in strange reversals of fortune, hard choices, unattractive tasks. This surrender, this demand for acceptance confidence and trust must reach our life of prayer, when we experience great emptiness and dryness.

Give us this day our daily bread: In the first part of the
Lord's prayer we are wholly concerned with God's
glory; in the second part we turn from the Infinite to
the finite and bring to God our earthly needs, we move
from adoration to petition. Here Our Lord's teaching
and practice are decisive: first the heavenly, then the
earthly. Seek first the kingdom of God, adore the
Father, and all the rest shall be added unto you. By
bread we ask for "the nourishment life requires -all
appropriate goods and blessings, both material and
spiritual" (CCC 2830); we acknowledge that in natural
and spiritual ways we depend on God, and ask both for
all that is necessary to live in this world and for all that
will sustain us in our journey towards the kingdom.
Some of the Fathers of the Church have also applied it
to the Eucharist. This prayer points to the identity of
the Giver and the Gift; in him and by him we live, and
our part is to be ready to receive him and accept him in
all the ways he feeds us.

And forgive us our trespasses, as we forgive: Our
growth in the life of prayer will bring with it a sharper
recognition of our share in the disorder of a fallen
world and our need of his mercy for our imperfections
and error, our shortcomings and excesses. The life of
prayer is always a progress in true humility. We are
always in need of the kindness and patience of God. But

if the petition begins with a confession of our wretchedness and his mercy, it goes on to make heroic demands on us: it looks to the future but our response must come first. Everyone that appeals to God's forgiveness has to move over to his side, as it were, to look with his eyes on human frailty and sin, to forget our own injuries, to recognise our common human frailty. Again and again in the Gospels we find Our Lord referring to the situation of the exacting, unforgiving one who dares to ask from God what he is not willing to give in return. It is for good reason that this petition appears at the end of Our Lord's lessons on prayer; it is the culmination of a life of worship, of union with the will of God, of awareness of a true filial relation to God and our true incorporation in the Body of Christ. "Forgiveness is the high point of Christian prayer; only hearts attuned to God's compassion can receive the gift of prayer" (CCC 2844). All this reminds us that the Lord's Prayer is a supernatural prayer, the prayer of those who exist to do God's will.

Lead us not into temptation, but delivers us from evil: As our life of prayer deepens, it brings with it a sense of God's personal guidance, protection and quiet action in our lives, as well as our weakness and inclination to sin. God himself tempts no one (*Jm* 1:12-13) but he does allow us to be tempted in order to probe our faith and faithfulness, and sometimes to educate. It is a revelation of our ways; in such moments we see whether God is the true rampart of our existence. How ready are we to follow God's lead everywhere even when we seem to be lost? Without passing through testing times, would we be able to answer this. Temptations and trials give us a chance to say yes to God; in the Bible that this kind of testing is a privilege of the Chosen People, reserved for those walking in God's paths. That's why James 1:2 and 1 Peter 1:6 understand testing to be a source of joy since temptation is God's way of taking us seriously. When we pray lead us not into temptation or make us not enter into the trial, we are not asking to be spared all situations of temptation and trial, which would mean coming to a complete standstill. We are confidently asking God not to abandon us to the power of evil at such a critical moment. Guard us from consenting to temptation; distance us from evil; do not let us be swamped by the struggles and confusions of the natural order. This is the teaching of one who knew temptation in the wilderness. Thus the prayer reminds us of the fragility of our nature and of the need to commit ourselves to God's power, to that personal relationship with him which is the ground of prayer and the remedy of temptation.

Trials in Prayer

Prayer is about a relationship; the aim of prayer is to deepen our relationship with God. Love desires the presence of the beloved, and so the person who prays places himself in God's presence. We must simply come and be in God's presence, as Bride and Bridegroom. This requires openness, and brings openness, an openness that does not seek to coerce God into responding as you think you would like. Anyone who loves feels himself breaking out of his own private world, but he has to be careful that he doesn't fall back to become self-seeking in his love. A lover can become self-seeking without being aware of it; he can aim only at his own enjoyment, using his partner as a means for this. He can use the material and spiritual goods of the other person till the day comes when he realizes that his love is gone, because he has been seeking himself all along. We mustn't seek to control and manipulate God in prayer, but open ourselves to him to become his servant and bride. Not to dominate but to serve, not to inflate the ego, but to transcend ourselves. We mustn't come to God hoping to experience something, hoping that something will happen to us. We must just come and be in his presence.

It is the contact with God that matters; all else is secondary and peripheral. This means that prayer is essentially a gift which we make of ourselves to God. It is all about giving and surrendering; it is not about feelings.

Absence

All the drama of the Song of Songs is here; the Bridegroom approaches and disappears, and to find him the Bride needs great patience, perseverance and conviction. Prayer must be pursued with a fidelity that characterises all love. He expects the pain of his apparent absence to be outweighed by love for him. Indeed real absence and real presence of God are equally good proofs of the concreteness of the relationship that prayer implies. It is important to see absence itself as a form of love, a mode of hope. Such were the experiences of the prophets, and of the Son of God on the Cross. It is a sign of selfless love if for the sake of those we love we are able to renounce things, to look beyond spiritual riches or delights. Love and friendship do not grow unless we are prepared to sacrifice a great deal for their sake. In the same way we must be prepared to put aside many things to give God first place.

Part of the reality of love is that it is free. Nothing is so free as love, and there is no freedom apart from love. It is very important to remember that both God

and we are free, and this freedom is of immense
importance because it is characteristic of real
relationships.

(Metropolitan Anthony Bloom)

If you think about it, most couples spend the greater
part of their life separate in their respective duties and
work. It is here that love must prove its strength. It
becomes loyalty, patience and humble service. In the
thought of his wife and children a man may bear with
emptiness and hardship of all kinds. For love of her
husband a wife endures weeks of loneliness at home
while he is away. All this is true of prayer. We must
really ask ourselves: do we really order our life
according to God's word, live in his divine love, and not
out of spiritual egoism and a desire for our own
spiritual enrichment or delight? Do we take our spousal
relationship seriously, our entering into a new and
eternal covenant, which alone makes possible this
interchange of love and life, which is the meaning of
prayer? Or is the bond with God valid only as long as
pleasure lasts?

We complain that He does not make Himself
present to us for the few minutes we reserve for Him,
but what about the twenty-three and a half hours
during which God may be knocking at our door, and

we answer 'I'm busy, I am sorry' or when we do not
answer at all because we do not even hear the knock
at the door of our heart, of our minds, of our
conscience, of our life.

(Metropolitan Anthony Bloom)

We must be very clear that the essence of
Christianity consists in fidelity freely given and
finally, persisting through all the difficulties of daily
life, aridity of spirit and even the seeming
remoteness of God.

(Hans Urs Von Balthasar)

Lack of feelings

Growth in prayer involves a weaning from a reliance on feelings as a criteria for prayer. The fact that prayer feels good does not mean that it is a real contact with God. We can be led astray by superficial sentiment. The feeling involved in prayer is different from the emotional impact of a film or novel. The experience of prayer is in the words of *The Cloud of Unknowing* is that of "a blind feeling unto God." Its energy does not come from sense impressions but from within. Prayer demands that we begin by distancing ourselves from emotional influence of external factors, and allow ourselves to be moved into a state of surrender and receptivity. Prayer is a most effective spiritual work and has its own reward, without the evidence of feelings.

Prayer is more than feelings. This is not to say that prayer has nothing to do with feelings, that how you feel is unimportant, but it does not tell you all you need to know about prayer. You may be feeling badly and God may be active; you may be feeling nothing in particular, but God may be very active; you may be feeling wonderful and that may have nothing to do with what God is doing. Thus a certain distance from feelings, not hostility to them or repression, but a realism about them, an ability to tell the difference between what God is doing and what you are feeling is the important thing. Neither bliss nor interior peace nor any feeling is equal to the hidden action of the Holy Spirit in one's soul.

It is not the experience of feelings that matter but the attitude with which we have to approach it. And that attitude is spousal: one of trusting, surrendering, self-giving. Prayer is a single-minded business. "The perfect apprentice asks neither to be spared pain, nor to be generously rewarded, nor asks indeed anything but God himself. He neither regards whether he is in pain nor in bliss, but only that the will of him whom one loveth is fulfilled" (*Cloud of Unknowing*). Feelings are in a way irrelevant. Only loving God has relevance. This is the attitude of the lover who is glad to give all, whose principal reward is in the giving, whose love is so strong it can dispense with the idea of getting. When writers on prayer speak this way they are not emotion-denying. They are not saying emotions or feelings are wrong; they are saying it is not needed in the work of prayer. Prayer is an activity way beyond our sense experience; the latter has nothing much to do with it by persuading us that nothing is happening at all. The whole thing is underpinned by love, and love is bound up with deepest movement of the heart and will, including and harmonizing all other movements and directing them Godwards. This results:

> *in a momentary disregard of one's personal concerns, the absence of self-centred thoughts. Feeling becomes prayer in the moment it forgets oneself and becomes aware of God. In prayer we shift the centre of living from self-consciousness to self-surrender.*
>
> (Abraham Heschel)

> *After a long spell of prayer, do not say nothing has been gained, for you have already achieved something. For after all, what higher good is there than to cling to the Lord, to persevere in unceasing union with him?*
>
> (St John Climacus)

Dryness or Spiritual Aridity

Spiritual dryness does not take away the power to pray or to persist in prayer. It only deprives one of the comfort or consolation one may have relied on in prayer. Bur if prayer ceases on the pretext of spiritual dryness or lack of comfort, then our spiritual life would soon founder. It would be wrong to stop praying during a time of dryness, because dryness is a living part of the very nature of prayer. If we accept it peacefully and with understanding, it can raise us to the higher stage of pure prayer, which is not based on emotion or incentives of any kind. The best thing to do is to accept aridity as part of the narrow way and carry on one's spiritual activity with calm and awareness.

In spiritual dryness we find that the soul is no longer able to receive comfort; it seems that grace has abandoned us. But all this is an experience external to one's will. The soul in its essence is one thing; and the emotion or lack of it proceeding from it is another. Thoughts, images, feelings may reveal the condition of the soul but they are not the soul nor do they represent it. Only our free will reveals and represents the soul. We are responsible for what our will chooses. Spiritual aridity is an experience external to one's will. Therefore the relationship between the soul and prayer can remain unchanged in spite of aridity, for dryness has nothing to do with the will. The activity of prayer can continue despite the experience of dryness. This is very important, for it exempts us from an imagined responsibility for our dryness. When comfort or interior pleasure cease, we tend to blame ourselves.

One of the major lessons of dryness is to teach us that prayer can continue without relying on consolation and emotional incentives. There is less danger of an inflated ego; we pray in order to please God not ourselves. It is an act of love for God, and therefore an act of bearing witness to our faith and love in Him. By this act of prayer which is sometimes difficult we show him that we prefer his will to ours. And we bear witness to greater love when we pray faithfully even at times when we lack desire. Not all meals are banquets, but if we go without it, we note the lack. It is the same with prayer. Being faithful, accepting what is given, we will grow in grace, humility and contentment. We must simply offer our prayer, and be ready for whatever God may give. As long as we have prayed attentively, truthfully and simply we have made a gift an offering of ourselves, and we can be sure God has accepted it. If we have done our best to give ourselves to God, it is always authentic and true. In this effort God sees a token of love, some response to his love. We can be sure that he will reward us in his own time and in his own way. Often it's only after prayer, not during it, that we reap fruits of what we have done. There is no question here of success or failure: prayer is always a success when we simply come with the intention to pray.[5] Existing prayers can be a help here. At moments of impasse the answer is not to withdraw but to stay in it. For there, at the very impasse, is the point where God will meet us to heal and save. That is the point where faith in prayer is being tested.

Pray with your whole being, though you feel nothing, though see nothing, even though it seems impossible to you. It is in dryness and in barrenness, in sickness and in feebleness that your prayer is most pleasing to me, even though you think it has little savour for you.

(Christ to Julian of Norwich)

Educative desolation does not in any way deprive the spirit of divine light. Grace hides its presence from the spirit in order to make it go forward, to have recourse in great fear and humility to God's help.

(Diadochus of Photike)

---

[5] Persistent non-feeling can be indicative of something, says M. Casey. It may be that the practices we are using are no longer fruitful; it can be a call to change. It may indicate a loss of dedication to a life of prayer. It may spring from a refusal to confront something negative in our lives. Prayer can be blocked if we are saying no to God in a particular area of our daily life, and refusing to admit that this is the case.

Distractions

Everyone who tries to pray becomes profoundly conscious of his inward multiplicity, disintegration, of his difficulty to concentrate himself on the present moment. Thoughts move restlessly through the mind, like the buzzing of flies (Bishop Theophan) or the leaping of monkeys or the "fool in the house" (St. Teresa of Avila). This lack of concentration, this inability to be here and now with the whole of our being, is one of the consequences of the Fall.

Instead of fighting these thoughts directly, monastic tradition suggests turning our attention away from them and looking elsewhere. The strategy here is not so much to empty our mind of what is bad but to fill it with what is good. As Barsanuphius and John of Gaza advise: "Do not contradict the thoughts suggested by your enemies, for that is exactly what they want and they will not desist. But turn to the Lord for help against them, laying before him your helplessness, for he is able to expel them and reduce them to nothing." *The Cloud of Unknowing* offers a similar 'spiritual dodge': "When you feel you are completely powerless to put these thoughts away, cower down before them like some cringing captive overcome in battle, and reckon that it is ridiculous to fight against them any longer. In this way you surrender yourself to God while you are in the hands of your enemies ... And this humility causes God himself to come down in his might, and avenge you of your enemies, and take you up, and fondly dry your spiritual eyes -just as a father would act towards his child."

It is clear that we cannot halt the inward flow of images and thoughts by an exertion of will-power. It is of little or no value to say to ourselves, "Stop thinking"; we might as well say "Stop breathing!" "The rational mind cannot rest idle," insists Mark the Monk. But although we cannot make the never-idle intelligence desist altogether from restlessness, what we can do is to simplify and unify its activity by repeating a short formula or prayer. The flow of images and thoughts will persist, but we shall be enabled gradually to detach ourselves from it. The repeated invocation of a Scripture text or the Jesus prayer will help us to 'let go' of the thought presented to us by our conscious or subconscious self. This letting go is what Evagrius and others had in mind when they spoke of prayer as a laying aside of thoughts -not a savage conflict, not a ruthless campaign of furious aggression, but a gentle, persistent act of detachment.

We should not think that our sinful or simply distracting thoughts, disqualify us from praying: the very act of prayer will purify them. In all this we make a double act of faith: an act of faith in God and also an act of faith in ourselves that there is a part of us which believes and loves and worships even if that part is not apparent to us. As the cry of someone who believes, prayer is always a powerful act of faith and generosity. This should enable us to keep a sense of perspective about distraction and other trials in prayer. Distractions don't matter in the end; they need not undermine the real intention. Prayer is not where the mind is but where the heart is.

Finally, it may be helpful to distinguish between prayer and ourselves as instruments of prayer. The instrument may be faulty but it is God who is the listener.

> *To stop the continual jostling of thoughts you must bind the mind with one thought, or the thought of One only.*
>
> (Bishop Theophan)

> *If you insist on not praying until you are freed from distraction, you will never pray; for distracting thoughts decline and disappear when we persist in prayer itself. He who seeks perfection before action and labour will achieve nothing ... God does not demand of man not to have thoughts at all passing through his mind while praying. Rather he demands that man pays no attention to them or relish them.*
>
> (Isaac the Syrian)

> *Hold on to the staff of prayer and you will not fall. And even a fall will not be fatal, since prayer is a devout, persistent, coercing of God (cf. Lk 18:5).*
>
> (St John Climacus)

From Words to Silence: The Prayer of the Heart and Contemplation

Words are important in prayer but after a time, they eventually become transparent. Once in a state of prayer, we may choose to leave aside the text, or stay with it only at a distance. This is a natural development. I use words to get started, I may stay with them but they may also become windows onto a deeper reality. When our gazing at God becomes more intense, we cease to notice the windows.

The Prayer of the Heart

The short prayers we have been describing are not to be said mechanically but with inward purpose and as a support. We concentrate our mind on the meaning of what we are saying. While starting as a prayer of the lips, as oral prayer, they grow with the course of time more inward, becoming prayer of the intellect or mental prayer. The sounds become less important, and may cease altogether; God is invoked silently, without any words, by the mind alone. Prayer becomes something offered by the mind and as well the lips - perhaps by the mind alone.

Finally, the intellect descends into the heart and is united with it, and so the prayer becomes a prayer of the heart, or as the ancients called it, a prayer of the mind in the heart. Heart here is to be understood in the biblical sense rather than in the modern sense, as signifying not just emotions and affectivity but the totality of the human person, the deepest and truest self made in the image and likeness of God. At this level prayer becomes the prayer of the whole person -no longer something we do or say but something we are. The ultimate purpose of prayer is not just a person who says prayers from time to time, but a person who is prayer all the time. At this stage, mind and heart are united in the act of prayer. The prayer of the heart is no longer something we just recite, but is part of ourselves. And so by God's grace, prayer comes to be something that says itself within us. Thomas of Celano described St Francis in this way: "In his whole being he was not so much a person who said prayers, as himself transformed into prayer" (*Life* 2:1). For Isaac the Syrian, this prayer is not so much our prayer as the prayer of Christ in us. It is a movement from the prayer which I say, to the prayer which says itself in me, or rather which Christ says in me. For in the spiritual life, heart has a double significance: it is both the centre of man's being and the point of meeting with God and man. It is both the place of self-knowledge where man discovers himself as he truly is and the place of self-transcendence, where man knows himself to be a dwelling of the Spirit, a temple of the Holy Trinity. Prayer of the heart, then, refers to the point where my action, my prayer become identified with the continuous action of Another in me. It is no longer prayer to Jesus but the prayer of Jesus himself.

This is not to say that the transition from oral prayer to prayer of the heart is rapidly accomplished. More commonly, those who recite the Jesus prayer or some other vocal prayer are granted from time to time special moments coming as a free gift, when the words of the prayer recede into he background and are replaced by a greater sense of God's presence and love. These short prayers begin as specific acts of prayer, but their eventual aim is to establish a state of prayer that is unceasing, that continues uninterrupted in the midst of other activities. No external condition , however distracting, is in itself incompatible with this inner prayer of the heart. "It may happen that the saints of God sit in the theatre and look at the deception of the world: but with their inner self they are talking with God (Macarius). "It was revealed to Abba Anthony in the desert: 'in the city there is one like you, a doctor by profession, who gives to those in need whatever he can spare; and throughout the whole day he sings the Thrice-Holy Hymn with the angels.'" Any of us with the help of the Spirit can imitate that doctor . The kingdom of God is within us. To pray is to enter this inner kingdom of the heart, and to stand before God and be conscious of his indwelling presence. Although the full glory of this Kingdom belongs to the age to come, we can all discover some part of its riches.

> *There are unfathomable depths in the heart... God is there with the angels, light and life are there, the kingdom and the apostles, the heavenly cities and treasures of grace: all things are there.*

(Macarius)

Contemplation

These short prayers begin as vocal prayers, but the rhythmic repetition enables the one who prays by the very simplicity of the words he uses to move beyond all language and images into the mystery of God. Cassian sees prayer as a progressive movement towards greater simplicity, more focused intention until at last a state of prayer is reached called the prayer of fire, "when the monk seeks to look to Jesus with the pure eyes of the soul" (X, 6). In this way, these short prayers develop, with God's help, into the prayer of loving attention or the prayer of the simple gaze where the soul rests in God. Contemplation is the soul's inward vision and the heart's simple rest in God. The essence of contemplation is extremely simple (which doesn't mean easy): an opening of the eyes of the mind and heart to God and the things of God, a preoccupation with God, the habitual disposition of being present to God. Both in Latin and Greek the word has the general meaning of gazing, wonder, the admiration of beauty, the consideration of wisdom. Perhaps the best definition of contemplation was given by the French peasant who described his way of prayer to the Curé d'Ars: "I look at Him, and He looks at me and we are happy together."

It is only in the Incarnation that God offers himself to human gazing in the supreme gift of His love (cf. 1 *Jn* 1:1,3). Christian contemplation is grounded in the absolute newness and wonder of the Incarnation, the union of human and divine, flesh and spirit. The "absence" of Jesus after the Ascension, the absence of vision in an earthly sense, makes possible a more intimate form of presence and seeing, a contemplation that sees and does not see at the same time, a seeing in faith and love: "All of us, gazing on the Lord's glory with unveiled faces, are being transformed from glory to glory into His very image by the Lord who is the Spirit" (*2 Cor* 3:18).

The object of all prayer is not an abstraction but a Divine Person; it is not a transient, subjective experience but the objective possession of God in His infinite reality and love. "To gaze is to love," wrote Dom Delatte. "Our whole soul is in our gaze." That is why contemplation is often described in the language of love and union: the soul can behold God without seeing Him, says St. Bernard, for it is already united to God as a wife is joined to her husband. The desire for God, expressed by this interior gazing, is already a genuine manner of possessing Him. Contemplation is not a product of relentless self-absorption and self-centred discipline; it is a going-out from self in love.

Indeed a great and divine and wonderful work is the soul ... He created it such as to be his bride and enter union with him so that he may inter-penetrate it and be 'one spirit' with it.

(Macarius)

Action and contemplation

The Incarnation, the perfect union of the divine and human, also provides the key for uniting our action and contemplation. The whole life of our Lord can be seen as an action that flows from the fullness of his heavenly and eternal contemplation and returns to it. Ever occupied with the vision of the Father, he nevertheless carried out his mission in time: "The Son only does what he sees the Father doing" (*Jn* 5:19). All that the Son does in his hidden life, public ministry and passion is the fruit of the original gazing upon the Father.

Because the tension between contemplation and action, abiding and going forth in love and obedience, has been overcome in Christ, it can be so in us too. It is possible to abide in God and go forth to a particular work. Those who would impose an artificial tension between action and contemplation forget that two people can love each other and yet pursue their respective activities. The lover is accompanied by the thought of his beloved in a way that does not impede his work but sustains it. How much more is this true of the soul and God, in whom it lives, moves and has its being. The believer lives a life of heaven on earth with the Beloved, lives it anew each day in prayer, the sacraments, the whole life of faith. When one's interior being has begun to be transformed by the habitual gazing at God, one develops a kind of response to God wherever encountered and no matter what the modality of His presence. We begin to see all things, persons and moments as signs and sacraments of God.

Thus the dichotomy between religion and the everyday round, between sacred and profane is over come. Contemplation is not a sudden irruption of the divine in total discontinuity with one's life, with everything that has gone before. It involves our looking at God and God coming to find us and meet us in response to our small, seemingly trivial fidelities. And this will result in a life more unified and whole, a deeply integrated life where liturgy, work, prayer, love and the service of one's neighbour are deeply interconnected and mutually enriching. The search for authentic prayer uses as its most fundamental raw material the everyday components of a life of faith and in time.

The whole of the Christian life consists in alternate periods of action and contemplation. Our goal should be to make the two interpenetrate more and more, to make our action more contemplative and our contemplation more active. Perfection is not a matter of choosing between obligations, of accepting one and rejecting the other, but of harmonising the two so that the whole of our life reflects and radiates our union with God, disclosing the inward divine meaning of action through a kind of co-working with God. For the saints, full of faith and open to the prompting of the Holy Spirit, action and contemplation are no longer distinguished: in the guest whom they feed, in the sick whom they serve, they "see" Christ. They see Christ present and acting in their brothers and sisters, in all that passes through their experience. There is no risk here of losing contemplation in an excess of action or of seeing action only from a human point of view. There can only be unified lives in which the leading direction, the priority, allows for detours -which is not the same thing as deviations. Such a continual abiding in God, gazing at God, resting in God is both the continual spur to right action and its ruling principle. Without this abiding, this gazing, our action is inclined to rush around, to take the form of a machine. Thus the person who in St. John's words "abides in my love" does not abandon himself to some kind of inert meditation, remote from the world, but draws his whole life from the very source of all action, God himself.

Give me a soul whose labours and leisure tend to rest in the presence of God.

(St. Bernard).

It is all the same to me whether you give yourselves to spiritual exercises or to the toil of exterior

62

labour, so long as your will is freely directed towards me.

(Our Lord to St. Gertrude)

Active contemplation

So far we have been looking at making action more contemplative, finding a contemplative dimension in our actions. But there is a real sense in which prayer is itself an action, an action whose fruit and extent cannot be measured or assessed; its ways are secret, not only secret from others but also secret from ourselves. The greater part of the fruit of our prayer and contemplation remains hidden with Christ in God.

The autobiography of St. Therese of Lisieux culminates in a celebration of this power of prayer: she compares it to the lever of Archimedes which is able to raise up the world; it sends up flowers to God which when passed through Our Lord's hands "receive immeasurable value," and "are strewn over the suffering Church." Pope John Paul II compares the power of contemplative prayer to those masters of the atom who fire rockets at a distance. This power of active contemplation belongs to every Christian, is realised by every Christian who participates in the fullness of the Christian vocation, the full-flowering of our baptism and the Christ-life in our souls. To be Christian must be, in a mysterious, but very real sense, a life fruitful for the Church, radiating out into the apostolate. "For the apostolate," Pope John XXIII reminds us, "in the true sense of the word consists in the salvific work of Christ, which is possible only through assiduous prayer and personal sacrifice... Hence it is that whoever endeavours to follow Christ in this essential aspect of his saving mission, even though he abstains from external action, exercises the apostolate in a most excellent way."

Prayer is opening oneself to the effective, invisible power of God. One can never leave the presence of God without being transformed and renewed in his being, for this is what Christ promised. The thing that can only be granted by prayer belongs to God (*Lk* 11:13). However such a transformation does not take the form of a sudden leap. It takes time. Whoever persists in surrendering himself to God in prayer receives more than he desires or deserves. Whoever lives by prayer gains an immense trust in God, so powerful and certain, it can almost be touched. He comes to perceive God in a most vivid way. Without ever forgetting our weakness, we become something other than we are.

This is the reason for prayer, the purpose of this spiritual marriage: the birth always of good works, good works.

(St Teresa of Avila, The Interior Castle)